New Horizons

Also by Cynthia Hallam and published by Ginninderra Press
Bread and Butter People
Rising to the Occasion
Town Life
Living in the Moment
Moving with the Times

Cynthia Hallam

New Horizons

Acknowledgements

'Mind Your Language' has appeared previously in *Writers' Voice*.

My enduring gratitude to
Trish Farmer for her fearless editorial comment
Greg Farmer for his cover and technical expertise
Ben Farmer for his patience with this technophobe
Deb Westbury for encouragement of self-belief
Christine Hayes, Warren Nicholls, Fran Fisher, Roz Vrielink
and Peter Miller for keeping our writing group inspired
Stephen Matthews for his faith in what I do

To Trish, Greg, Michael and Ben with love
and in fond memory of Marie

New Horizons
ISBN 978 1 76041 326 2
Copyright © text Cynthia Hallam 2017
Cover: Greg Farmer

First published 2017 by
GINNINDERRA PRESS
PO Box 3461 Port Adelaide 5015 Australia
www.ginninderrapress.com.au

Contents

The Triumvirate	7
Nightfright	8
Promises, Promises	10
Coming to Terms	12
Claude	13
Mind Your Language	14
Flying under the radar	16
Acceptance	17
Traffic	18
New Horizons	19
Steam	20
Cultural Pressures	21
Commerce	22
Trouble	24
Caprice	25
Disconnection	27
Fitting In	29
A Sign of the Times	30
The Reality of Lawns	31
Fate	32
In Memoriam	33
Keeping up Traditions	34
Perversity	35
Carnage	36
Retailing	37
Persuasion	38
Longing	39
Transition	40
Sold!	41
The Evangelists	42

Catchat	44
Weather	45
In a Midnight Garden	46
The Curiosity	47
Metamorphosis	48
On the Spectrum	49
Diversity	50
Moments	51
Cold Comfort	52
Done Over	53
The Aria	54
The Dream Catcher	55
A Seasonal Routine	56
Classified	57
Mrs Downer	58
Frustration	59
Contact	60
The Bond	61
Tuning In	62
A Very Satisfying Encounter	63
Wishful Thinking	64

The Triumvirate

We relax on the veranda, me, myself and I,
enjoying breakfast coffee
watching the regulars parade along the street.
The elderly man and his geriatric dog
shuffling along on six arthritic legs.
The middle-aged jogger with a heart-attack paunch
sweating the possibility.
That skinny bloke with the long, shaggy beard
battling to knot a plastic bag
as his canine goliath tows him to the park.

Clusters of kids shambling to school
collectively detached from any personal interaction,
eyes and fingers focused on their palms.
The dawdling woman, absorbed in her phone
while her poodle checks its weemails
at every pole and gate.
The young couple fuelled by private smiles
behind the power-walking trio, all arms pumping.

So, the neighbourhood has now begun its day
and the time has come
to be getting along with my own predictable routine,
content, that in the absence of any others,
the three of us are good company for each other.

Nightfright

I am floating,
blind and feather light
beneath
a crushing canopy.
Something indefinable
pulses against my skin
to the tempo
of my laboured breath
and is filtering
through my brain,
defying comprehension.

I am flying,
lost in outer space.
A galaxy of thoughts
take a tentative hold
but dissolve
before they can
disengage
the magnetic force
that is drawing me
screaming to oblivion.

I am drowning
in an all-engulfing tide
until reason
resuscitates my senses
and I struggle awake
gasping, sweating
as if I'm stumbling
across the finish line
of a marathon,
heartbeat ragged
and pumping its relief.

Promises, Promises

As usual, they have promised
that they will take me for a walk
when they get home
if I am good while they're away,
so I didn't bite the meter man,
just gave a warning growl
and grabbed the bottom of his jeans
because I'm being good today.

I've been weeing on the orchids
instead of killing off the grass.
Alerting all the neighbours
to any movement in the street.
I dismembered the local paper
and buried it in the lawn
for tidying up the environment
is a virtue hard to beat.

And while that Labradoodle
was watching through the gate,
the chance was there to show her
that this stud would be a gift,
but I jumped about inside the fence
to exhibit my credentials,
instead of out and over
(if you are following my drift!)

I did not bark at the postman,
only gave his hand a nudge
as he was reaching for the letter box
yet his words were so unfair.
I kindly showed the pup next door
my personal technique
for taking washing off the line
with just a minor tear.

So I've really tried to be righteous
until the family gets back home
when they'll get a robust welcome
with a good old bark and wag.
I'll bring them in an orchid plant
to prove where I have been
and reckon once I ditch this shirt
that walk is in the bag.

Coming to Terms

It isn't easy letting go of what might have been.
The dreams born to wither on the vine
and left to perish by our own inaction.
Those opportunities missed by complacency
and indefensible naivety.
Good times taken for granted then wasted
mourning other, unfulfilled expectations.
The resentment spawned when our decisions
took us in the wrong direction
on the poor advice of others
instead of trusting our own intuition.
The broken heart that never quite healed.

So today I am making peace with my past
and the true purpose of my existence can begin.
I have brushed away
the clinging hand of my history.
Cast bitter memories into the wilderness
and let the positives prevail,
realigned my focus to appreciate more
the value of the here and now.
My future will be what I choose to make it,
a blank canvas, that until this moment,
has been waiting in the wings
for my attention.

Claude

As usual, we are all aware
that he has entered the room.
He has a full bottle personality,
an air of confidence
that anyone would envy.
A larger-than-life magnetic aura
that renders forgivable
his belief in feline superiority.

Satisfied that he has engaged
our undivided attention,
he settles on the mat,
juggles with beguiling expertise
the woolly toy
knitted for his birthday
until dues paid, he flicks it away
to bask in our admiration.

With the sphinx-like demeanour
of a poker player
he assesses all options,
springs onto the chosen lap
and circles into his comfort zone
with a rumbling purr,
exhausted by the magnitude
of his benevolence.

Mind Your Language

I don't understand
how the sky can be blue
yet we can be feeling blue.
Antagonists can stack on a blue
or wonder what in the blue blazes
is going on and scream blue murder.
A redheaded man is nicknamed 'Blue'.
All true!

A road between two mountains is a pass.
You can pass an exam or pass the buck.
We can pass the time or pass the jam.
You can pass out or can pass away.
A new admirer can make a pass,
can pass you by or pass you up
or win a family movie pass.
What a farce!

Blocks are squares of streets or buildings.
Are a piece of land or a piece of wood.
You can have your block knocked off
(or something you own knocked off.)
Producers block an action on a set.
You can reside in a block of units
and block someone else's view.
Kids like to play with blocks
but polish off an ice block.
What a crock!

Cricket is played on a pitch.
It is quite easy to pitch a tent.
Roads are repaired with pitch
yet mountain roads have pitch.
It is great when helpers pitch in.
Rivals can't wait to pitch a battle.
A boat's pitch can make you sick.
Singers need to have perfect pitch.
You can pitch a ball and pitch a line,
pitch your manuscript to a publisher.
You can even have your pitch queered.
How weird!

Think about fast and litter,
graft, plot, wearing and sound,
ring and smart, medium and race
sock and harbour, crook and draw.
The English language is as clear as mud.
What a dud!

Flying under the radar

It wasn't as if he was small in size.
His unobtrusive demeanour
simply made no impact.
Attracted no interested attention.

His features were pleasant enough,
just short of being handsome.
His build, while not athletic,
was in reasonable shape.
His clothes were never too trendy
or seen better days
so he always blended in.

He worked somewhere in the city.
Would quietly lend a hand,
be the 'extra man' at dinners,
make up the numbers for a game.
He paid for his round of drinks
after the footy.
Gave lifts to the lady next door
and mowed her lawn.

He succumbed to a heart attack
only months before he retired
but few attended his service.
Someone from Human Resources,
sitting at the back,
constantly checking his watch
and a small, white haired woman,
eyes closed,
sifting through her memory
for the neighbour's name.

Acceptance

On a park bench bathed in sunlight,
the old couple are holding hands
like teenagers on a first date,
his smile etched by love and expectation.
Tenderly, he caresses her cheek
to maintain her transient attention
and is rewarded with the twinkle in her eye
that had captured his heart so easily
all those years ago.

Her thoughts hover on butterfly wings,
tantalising and full of promise
then, 'Hello, Ted. It's nice of you to come,'
and he basks in the cherished moments
of fleeting recognition
before they skitter off into thin air,
perhaps to take refuge with the roses,
their vibrant presence already diminished
by afternoon shade.

Traffic

The highway seems much busier today.
Waiting to cross, my frustration simmers in overdrive
as I watch an armada of mechanical behemoths charging by,
drivers hypnotised by distance and fatigue,
intent on beating the lights further down the road
until a progressive, shattering chorus of airbrake angst
diminishes their hopes of a scheduled delivery.

I seize my opportunity to sprint across
to the small cluster of local shops, but timing askew,
I shelter half way on the pedestrian retreat,
not quick enough to outrun the conga line of traffic
approaching at increasing speed from the other direction.

Above the scramble, noise and fumes,
a rabble of complaining cockatoos perform a high wire act
on the power lines, until some private avian signal
sets them flapping, en masse, to the haven of the park,
leaving me to deal with one of the major irritations
in the contemporary lives of humans.

New Horizons

As the fireworks spectacular closes out the year,
we can find ourselves reflecting on our lives
since the previous, annual extravaganza.
The resolutions realised or not.
Undertakings languishing in disappointment
or forging ahead at full throttle.
Relationships that have floundered or flourished,
the lingering pain of ill-advised mistakes
or the satisfying rewards of our successes.

But with the sky ablaze in a last fiery shower,
the old year has departed,
its replacement is now landing in our laps
and whether we are ready or not
the time has come to start navigating
this new, unpredictable chapter of our history,
leave our unique footprints in virgin sand
to fuel next year's expected evaluation.

Steam

The commute from the city is long
and the carriage is silent,
the view outside too familiar for most
to engage in much observation.
Headphones centre concentration,
electronic toys lure nimble fingers.
Pages of Sunday papers quietly turn
in deference to the repose of others
until beyond the window's scratched glass
a mystery hijacks consciousness
as another overpass comes into view
fringed with eager faces
and photographers checking their focus.

The crowd waiting at the next station
shows little interest in their arrival
for a rumbling in the other direction
has claimed its attention.
A steam train is puffing up to the platform
like a giant friendly dragon
lustily acknowledging its reception.
Their own carriage comes alive,
passengers flocking to the windows
sharing their delight,
the smiles and chatter lasting
until they reach their destinations,
exchanging waves as the magic lingers.

Cultural Pressures

From the wading pool
shrieks of delight greet random gushes of water
from the gaping mouths of concrete fish,
splashes from the dunking end of the slide,
mermaids flapping imaginary tails.
Parents are encouraging toddlers to swim,
babies introduced to floating.
A man and his two small sons
are playing around in the thick of it,
enjoying the summer holiday afternoon.

From a bench under the trees
the mother and daughter are watching
swathed in scarves and modest ankle skirts,
the woman's Madonna-like face
serene with uncomplaining acceptance,
but the young girl
mourning a promised new and better life
is observing with wistful eyes,
hands folded demurely in her lap,
the impact of lifelong compliance dawning.

Commerce

The new shopping centre has just opened
replacing the cluster of friendly shops
that was the beating heart
of our neighbourhood
and sadly, the national chains have taken over.
Aldo's Fruit and Veg, the newsagency,
Ted's grocery and Madge's deli
are now but a fond memory.
The chemist, familiar with all our ills
has been displaced by a massive pharmacy
with ads on the telly.
The best fish and chips ever fried
have been supplanted
by a confusion of disparate alternatives.
Security cameras will record our every move.
It is diabolical!

All of our objections to its construction
were totally ignored.
We've been set adrift in the impersonal world
of greedy, self-interested commerce,
the long and comfortable history
of our unique corner of the universe
just another anonymous casualty
of modern living!
But oh! The luxury and convenience
of a proper car park, hairdresser and ATM!
The trendy coffee shop
and a branch of that famous city store!
Well, on second thoughts
maybe I'll drive back over
and check out the rest of the opening specials,
forget about eating any humble pie
and try a kebab.

Trouble

The violence of the movie
engulfs the intimacy of the theatre,
a cheap drug for the young delinquents
yahooing in the back row.
A demonic midget with a warped brain
is spraying mass obliteration
but is obviously playing favourites
for the hero, and semi-naked heroine
with the promise-everything eyes
are miraculously spared
as one by one
their gallant band of warriors is slain,
the brutality of their demise
gratifying high-octane expectations
until the villain's head is blown away
and the couple embrace.

Released by the credits,
the boisterous youths surge outside
into the late night temptations
of the city street,
hormone wired and impatient to fulfil
some of their new, exciting fantasies.
To demonstrate, like the hero,
their own invincibility.

Caprice

Well past the equinox
the spring weather
is still unpredictable.
The threats and promises
of all seasons in a day
have confused the azaleas,
a frosty breeze teasing
bud-laden branches
on the cusp of
their annual mass display.

Sadly, the freesias,
those usual harbingers
of salubrious weather
appear to have given up
before they can be
brought inside
to delight our senses,
enhance the illusion
that it is getting warmer.

But the maple tree
is sprouting new leaves.
The grass and days
are a little longer.
Magpies are returning
from wintering elsewhere
to check the birdbath
is still in working order
so perhaps by tomorrow,
this lingering chill
will be just a memory
and deliverance
is one more shiver away.

Disconnection

After a long association with
the service station up the road
I have been caught up
in the march of changing times.
The counter's cheerful jumble
of cheap sunglasses,
cigarette lighters and sweets
has been banished and replaced
with a security screen.

Bandit proof, the proud owner
demonstrates its quality,
indicates a camera on the ceiling
in addition to the one outside
and I realise, that from now on,
filling up will never be the same.

This new regime is stalling
our usual friendly interaction,
catching up with the local gossip
or airing my opinion
now seeming much too private
to be recorded for posterity.

With cupboard doors saving me
from nicotine temptation,
our transaction is conducted
through a slot in the screen
and I hastily retreat
to the sanctuary of my car,
release the immobiliser's grip
lamenting this latest assault
on the fabric of my wellbeing.

Fitting In

It is just an ordinary street,
conservative, average suburban
I suppose the purists would say.
A collection of renovated bungalows,
double fronted bricks
and several, upgraded to two stories.
The lawns are regularly cut,
gardens reasonably neat
and the children playing outside
are, as a rule, well behaved and polite.

But smack bang in the middle,
new owners have painted their house
in a what were they thinking of blue.
With a matching fence!
Passers by can't help noticing
the canary-yellow blinds
being installed in the front windows,
supervised outside by the couple,
oblivious it would seem,
of the whispered umbrage in the street.

Yet who would believe it?
Their wolfhound is wagging its tail
and is surprisingly friendly.
The mower and box of new shrubs
waiting on the veranda are reassuring
and their enthusiastic greetings
are so genuinely warm that
integration into the neighbourhood
may be much smoother than
might otherwise have been expected.

A Sign of the Times

For the first time since the fad began,
no Trick or Treaters
have come to my door on Halloween.
The waiting basket of chocolates
has remained untouched.
No laughing ghouls
have paraded along the street.
No parents hovered at the front gate
while skeletons and princesses
marched across the lawn
as we grown-ups exchanged waves.

It seems that without my realisation,
the local kids have all grown up,
amused now by electronic devices
with limitless virtual distractions
so I turn off the porch light,
demolish a chocolate or two
and accept that the passage of time
has redefined
the dynamics of the neighbourhood,
that from now on,
any future participation is unlikely.

The Reality of Lawns

Accustomed to air-conditioned travel
to an air-conditioned school,
some summer weekends will find him
outside cutting the grass
as directed, so unreasonably, by his father.
Today, he is absolutely convinced
that on his weekly afternoons of sport
the weather is never as hot
as when he's sweating his way down the back
to empty a catcher onto the compost heap
or heaving aside the stupid garden seats
cluttering up the lawn.

Spurred on by the seductive appeal
of his devices inside,
he finishes a bottle of water on the front step
and summons up his strength
for a final assault on the roadside verge.
Takes the shower demanded by his mother
then bolts to the sanctuary of his room
where with one easy click of a finger,
his real world is waiting.

Fate

Ted knew the writing was on the wall
when he discovered that he was too old
to take out a funeral plan.
Sure, he still played a solid game of bowls,
walked every day
and goes to the club on Friday nights
where Gladys brings him lamingtons
and gives him the eye during the bingo.
But even so,
it certainly made a bloke start to think.

He reckoned that his marbles were still
in good working order.
If he was asked to sort out a problem
with a neighbour's dicky mower
he did it without any trouble.
His licence has not been restricted
so he can drive his prized old Holden
whenever and wherever he wants to go,
even though
the traffic seems to be getting faster.

Until now, he's been more than content
but perhaps it was time to break away
from his boxed-in routine.
Try the meal deals at the other club,
get one of those mobile phones
and sign up for that Seniors' Club outing
to Jenolan Caves including buffet lunch
that Gladys kept carrying on about.
After all,
there was no point in dying wondering.

In Memoriam

They cluster
in the middle of the road
where one of their own
lies unmoving,
a shredded wing raised
in surrender to the traffic.
With nothing behind,
I slow to a stop,
allowing their mourning
to run its course
until a strident horn
jars me from my reverie
and I drive forward
gently
until they all take flight,
heading for the bush
to restore
their equilibrium.

Keeping up Traditions

Much too soon, the season is over.
The moulting tinsel tree is packed up,
decorations returned to cardboard boxes
with faded, peeling labels.
Garlands, eased from unstable hooks
by fragile, arthritic fingers
have been neatly coiled ready for storage,
the front door wreath brought in.

Finally, she gathers up the cards,
revisits the friendly greetings from long ago
then secures them with a ribbon
for display next year,
her thoughts wrapped in memories of
rituals shared before her world moved on,
the time-honoured traditions
that these days, she celebrates alone.

Perversity

The towering agapanthus stems are sagging
at half-mast, completing their summer display,
lavender orbs already reducing to seed.
The grass has acquired such a brittle persona
that the resident blue-tongue lizards
are hesitating to cross to the water bowl
located beneath the birdbath for their benefit.

The heat and humidity have reached their peak,
energy is being sapped and sleep deprived
but the sky seems to be promising some relief
and will hopefully preclude the prospect
of another, enervating session with the hose,
impatient for the cool and damp of winter,
ignoring that as usual I'd be pining for summer.

Carnage

As always, a law unto themselves
and completely disregarding my presence,
the cockatoos have arrived for their annual feast.
Above, the canopy of my peach tree flinches
as each treat is looted then discarded
with barely a nibble gone,
bombarding me with a callous insensitivity.

I shout at the hooligans and brandish my rake
but they just carry on, squabbling with each other
as they gorge on their pilfered repast.
Drop the odd calling card
delivering their opinion of my futile defence.

Fed up with the waste and the mess,
I resolve to invoke the principle that might is right
and with the deepest regret
must now deploy the final shot in my arsenal.
I will uproot my beloved old tree and replace it
with a flowering peach memorial,
trusting that the last laugh
will be satisfying enough to restrain my tears.

Retailing

The aisles of the town's new supermarket are packed.
Shoppers with laden trolleys are battling for space to move,
noise level reaching the stratosphere.
Exhortations to check out the red-hot opening specials
are competing with music, psychologically oozing well-being.

Two over-excited small girls are shrieking petulant complaints
as they are bundled past shelves of enticing treats
until a wandering clown placates them with balloons.
An elderly couple are bickering about her biscuit choice
oblivious to the others, impatient to reach their selections.
A young couple with a sleeping baby are yawning
as they contemplate a bewildering array of infant paraphernalia
until the child wakes up and begins to cry
when some youths push by, no purchase in mind
but making the most of their exciting new diversion.

At the front door, a man wearing a suit and a welcoming smile
observes the register queues with satisfaction and relief
for like all his multinational's recent incursions,
its well-researched and optimistic bottom line projection
does not appear to be in jeopardy.

Persuasion

The ad breaks on the telly are getting longer.
Fast food entices and work-hungry utes
are threatening to wreck their suspensions.
Airlines tempt travel to over-hyped locations.
Our budgets can be managed, debt free forever.
Mortgages can be provided on better terms
than those locked in already.
Supermarket specials coax a thrifty conversion
from our usual shopping routine.

My choice of toothpaste is obviously wrong.
The health fund enjoying my loyalty for years
is offering new clients a better deal than mine.
Access to our electronic devices can be bundled
into all manner of cheaper confusions
then surely, not again! that overkilled promo
for that shameless reality fiasco.

Just as our overloaded brains are drowning,
the battle of ideas finally reaches a conclusion
when we are spared more badgering by the news
and no one is trying to sell that!

Longing

For a moment she closes her eyes for some respite
from the relentless, glaring screen.
The clamour of the office recedes into a void
and he is there, with the knowing smile
he shares only with her.

She sees him every day
through the glass wall of his sanctuary,
and knows she must be patient
until the time is right to share their secret.
Let the world know
of their passionate attraction.

She hears his door sliding open
and waits with delicious anticipation for his attention
but as usual, his greeting is not for her.
The woman from accounts
returns his smile and they leave for lunch
in intimate conversation.

She sighs, refocusing on the screen
while once again, her enduring illusion is shattering,
disappearing into the distance
like a favourite book left on the train
and speeding out of reach.

Transition

The early winter days are closing in.
Only weeks ago,
sunsets bathed our evenings in a vibrant, rosy glow
enhancing our feelings of wellbeing.
The leaves have surrendered to their fate,
bare branches, stark against the sky,
mourning the loss of their brilliant autumn finery.
Birds are departing to warmer climes,
dog-walkers moving faster
to beat the fading light and burgeoning chill.

So for a while, the grass won't need to be cut,
the mower can be serviced and put away.
Weeds have slowed their assault,
gardens not require extra watering.
But the time has come to prune the shrubs,
chop firewood, rake up leaves,
cosset plants through hostile frosts
for the reality is that Mother Nature's in control,
and we mortals ever her slaves.

Sold!

The auctioneer slaps his palm
and points to the family hugging each other
on the periphery of the hopeful and the curious
crowding the footpath.
In the front window, behind lace curtains,
the elderly woman is relieved
that the home that had nurtured three generations
would be appreciated and well looked after
by such a nice family.

She imagines the children playing backyard cricket,
climbing up the mulberry tree
when the rope ladder is repaired.
Absorbed in school-holiday make-believe
in the cubby her husband built
once their father has it back in shape.
Playing board games and Snap! on rainy days,
their happy shrieks echoing along the veranda
and her mind is set at rest,
the prospect of a future somewhere else
much less distressful.

The auctioneer and the parents are conferring,
young ones distracted by something in their palms
so content at last,
she wanders through the rooms one final time
sealing family history into her memory,
oblivious of the reality
that contemporary life has passed her by
and blissfully unaware of the For Lease sign
waiting in the wings.

The Evangelists

A kookaburra choir
surprises me
this chilly morning
and I wonder
what has prompted
their performance.

Was it my own
fumbling attempts
at scraping frost
from the windscreen
of my car
with stiff, icy fingers
when it is obvious
from their view,
that unfettered
by such distractions
I could simply fly?
Has that poodle
being walked
in a knitted jumper
tickled their fancy
or just singing
from the heart
for the joy of living?

I listen, smiling now
and attack my task
with renewed vigour,
reminded
that irksome
as it sometimes is,
life is still better
than the alternative.

Catchat

A blood-curdling shriek alerts the neighbours
that Oscar has called in to visit the girls.
He sits on the back porch, huge, imposing,
confident that his dazzling, ginger stripes
are still semaphoring macho appeal.

Despite a lack of interest in romance,
the smaller sister exchanges caterwauls
with their handsome visitor
from behind the safety of the screen door,
almost nose to nose through the wire
but the other, much bigger yet more timid,
has swiftly retreated
to her fallback position behind a chair
pretending to bathe an immaculate paw,
content to leave the ranting to others.

I block my ears to the escalating din
until the explosive racket runs out of steam,
Oscar's tail flicking in frustration.
With a final screech to send him on his way
my sweet and gentle companion
withdraws demurely to her favourite chair
for a leisurely bath and another nap,
reassured no doubt
that regardless of the passing years,
her mojo remains in good working order.

Weather

Late in the morning,
the local park is virtually empty.
Persistent rain has kept away the family picnics
and cheerful, squabbling cricket matches
celebrating Father's Day
dusted with the magic of belonging.

Alone and with downcast eyes
a man walks the path through dripping greenery,
shoulders hunched in dismal isolation,
wind threatening to blow out his umbrella,
until without any warning
the relentless squalls evaporate,
a hint of sunlight illuminates the horizon
with the promise of a better day ahead
and somehow,
whatever heartache consumed his thoughts
appears to have been resolved.

Umbrella furled he turns, retraces his steps,
smiling now and head held high,
observing the gardens with apparent pleasure,
noting perhaps,
that despite the recent adverse weather
they are still giving birth to a brilliant display
and maybe like them, he has moved on,
memories of his journey to the far side of reason
swept away with the rain.

In a Midnight Garden

In the torchlight,
a pair of eyes are sparkling gems,
unfathomable, all knowing,
mesmerising an unsuspecting innocent
before the satisfying conclusion
only hunting felines can appreciate.
In the moon-shadowed canopy of eucalypts
a rustling, a faint murmur hang in limbo
then dissolve into the deep silence
of sleep and covert vigilance.

A leaf paraglides to the grass below
and safely cushioned by a first hint of dew
flaunts the freshness of its beauty
like a princess in a fairy bower
awaiting rescue by a handsome prince
from whatever perils lie ahead.
At the boundary fence a twig snaps
fraught with the essence of possibility
yet profound stillness follows.

Caught in a vacuum, time is immobilised,
imagination freeze-framed
until somewhere else in the neighbourhood
a barking dog is admonished
and a distant train rumbles to the plains
restoring the existence of other places,
other lives that are still evolving in the dark,
a reminder, that a bright new day
will soon be open for business.

The Curiosity

What has it witnessed
this candle,
now a ghost of itself,
its beauty spent
in the service of others?
A profession of faith,
a lovers' tryst,
a commemorating vigil,
an important dinner?
Perhaps as saviour
in a crisis
when other illumination
was not an option.
But what of its future,
this candle,
now but a stub of wax
and a charred wick,
devoid of any former
elegant credentials?
Discarded,
abandoned out of sight
as a worn-out relic
or lovingly preserved
in remembrance
of a time gone by,
destiny now in the eye
of its current beholder.

Metamorphosis

Barely mid-spring, an insurgent heatwave
has surprisingly attacked,
the temperature already uncomfortably high.
Azaleas at the peak of their brilliant display
are giving up the ghost and wilting
beyond any chance of miraculous redemption.
The water in the birdbath is evaporating.
Lizards out hunting caught unawares
are lying comatose in the shade
and bushfire alerts are now being broadcast
well in advance of the usual routine.

So I've put away the gardening paraphernalia
for today's onslaught on the weeds,
postponed the power walk around the park
and cancelled my usual trek to the shops
until hopefully, tomorrow's forecast reprieve.

Fans have been geared to jet velocity,
the household pets sprawling underneath,
so I think I'll settle down with my library book
and a nice, refreshing iced coffee
which I suppose, when I come to think of it,
isn't a bad alternative to my planned agenda.

On the Spectrum

Having had no choice in the lottery of life
he views the world from a different perspective,
his fast-flowing thoughts often bursting from left field
so that for a moment, you find yourself floundering,
not quite sure if they are based on wisdom or naivety.
Half boy, half man and quite often the complete charmer,
his speech is formal and mature beyond his years,
smile rendering forgivable any lapse from verbal grace
with words not in his special school's curriculum.

No matter where a conversation is heading
it is diverted to something already claiming his attention
with a dogged persistence that can be disconcerting
and with the best of intentions may advise from memory
the timetable of the local bus for your information.
He can be stubborn, super-glued into his daily routine
unaware of any need to comply with others' expectations
yet sometimes conforms with impressive capability.

At random, he can be frustratingly obtuse,
kind, quirky, lovable and loving, forgetful, outrageous,
brilliantly wise, a pain in the neck or an absolute delight,
but always uniquely himself. Just like everyone else.

Diversity

As usual the evening news
is a microcosm of life
in a complex universe.
Overseas,
earthquakes and tornados
claim hundreds of lives,
government buildings
are blown up by
self-destructing zealots
causing tragic losses,
two posturing leaders
are ramping up aggression.
Masses seek refuge
from civil wars,
sport officials disgraced.

At home,
proposed budget cuts
and tax reforms
are being condemned,
bushfire alerts upgraded,
drought relief
under consideration,
councils under scrutiny.
A town launches
its weight loss scheme,
a bikie war has erupted,
city traffic is in chaos
and in breaking news,
a football star
needs surgery on a finger.

Moments

Our lives are full of small ripples of pleasure.
Like finding a current magazine in the waiting room.
When a parking spot opens up just ahead of you
in a packed shopping mall.
Observing the dawning smile on a doctor's face
as he scans your test results.
Opening a gift that is exactly what you wanted.
Grasping in your hand your mislaid keys
when time and mobility are of the essence.

Fending off a loved pet's excited welcome home
after a day of feeling unappreciated.
Smelling the first gardenia bloom of the season.
Opening a power bill that is much less than expected.
The mechanic ticking off your ageing car's rego
with nothing major requiring attention.

These fleeting, warm and fuzzy frissons of delight
should be recognised as life's little bonuses
to be stored away in our memory for comfort later on
when sometimes, life isn't quite so benevolent.

Cold Comfort

Further up the mountain,
snow has been falling overnight
and we join the crawl of weekend traffic
to witness this rare phenomenon.
We travel with caution on familiar roads
rendered almost alien
as edges blur into the shrouding mist
fuelling our rising excitement.

Finally, we reach our destination
and the driver, no stranger to snow like us,
heads across to the takeaway
as we novices race towards the park
eager to be throwing snowballs
like they show on the evening news
but the early-winter sun
has already wreaked havoc on the dream
that is evaporating before our eyes.

With the remnants of fervent anticipation,
we scoop up handfuls of residual frost
but it seeps through our fingers
onto the ground, and not even hot chips
can appease our disappointment.

Done Over

Well, here I am,
the only house in the street left in its original condition.
AND IT'S NOT MY FAULT! I'm just a victim of circumstance.
For some time, my guttering has needed attention,
a paint job is well overdue, the garden an embarrassment.
No second story has been added, new blinds installed
or a patio and barbecue area extended out the back.
The front fence was never replaced to enhance my charm.
It's so obviously unfair!

First of all, my owners retired to swan around Australia
(in a caravan called 'Getinaway' for heaven's sake,)
and couldn't afford the extra expense of doing me up.
The next were transferred overseas, decided to stay on
but couldn't be bothered with long-distance repairs
so uncaring of my feelings, threw me to the wolves 'as is'.
This latest mob are just cashing in on the real estate boom.
Heartless, all of them!

So unloved, I languish here, hearing that I'm too overpriced,
and my kitchen and bathroom are 'seriously off the planet'
as all and sundry traipse through, making hurtful remarks
about my orange feature walls and lovely floral carpets
then walk away, unimpressed and uninterested
with absolutely no appreciation of my future possibilities.
A total injustice, isn't it!

The Aria

Through the new sun room's open door,
mother magpie is searching for the garden bed
that was a hunting ground for generations,
but unfamiliar with the house's recent addition,
she beats her wings against its walls of glass
in baffled distress
while her babies below shriek with impatience
for the morsels that are not yet forthcoming.

Trapped in a corner, she evades all efforts
to direct her to the freedom of the open door
until finally, panting with exhaustion
she is momentarily still, so carefully I approach,
cup her trembling body in my hands,
supporting her while her heart slows down
before setting her free and she ushers her family
to the sanctuary of the hedge.

But just before sunset overtakes the day,
a fluttering outside on the new porch railing
gains my attention and mother magpie is singing,
gifting the most enchanting moment of my life
when I realise, with disbelieving delight,
that her magical performance is just for me.

After a final glorious trill she swoops away,
hopefully aware that the only thanks she can give
were received with heartfelt appreciation.

The Dream Catcher

In the shop window,
a confection of feathers beads and glitter
shimmers in the afternoon sun,
dismissed as an amusing indulgence
yet still managing to hold our rapt attention.

Is it reactivating dormant dreams?
Prodding thoughts of fantasised aspirations
into genuine contemplation?
Sparking notions of finding a new love
or that the impossible may just be possible?
Is it taking in the private longings
that we are unable to share with others?

The shopkeeper carefully wraps up
our fragile new, undervalued psychologist,
tucking inside an unexpected bonus
of inspired imagination.

A Seasonal Routine

At last it is really spring.
The pair of crimson rosellas
have returned
and strutting their stuff
over the back lawn's first cut
since winter lost its bite.

They come every year,
feathered splendour
stark
against the fresh greenery,
eyes alert for the old cat
who watches every move
but relocated
to the cattery in the sky
last autumn.

Classified

Alas, as the digital world takes over,
the ads in the local paper are shrinking,
but are still an insight into the reality
of our everyday existence.

Tradies and handymen are ready to go,
cultural aspirations catered for.
Births and engagements are announced,
the deceased taken care of
by funeral directors, celebrants
and auctioneers who liquidate estates.
A clairvoyant 'acclaimed for accuracy'
can predict your future,
another find the skeletons in your past.

Pets are always well represented.
The kittens that are free to good homes,
budgies that have flown the coop.
Dog whisperers will come to the door
and turn your tearaway into an angel.
A mobile vet will sort out emergencies.

The items 'For Sale' may be fewer
but garage sales still foster speculation
on the 'bric-a-brac' or the redundant
and look! Someone's getting rid of
a double bed and two bikes.
Are they splitting up or slowing down?
And guess what? Just around the corner!

Mrs Downer

With the best intention in the world,
she sees herself as the neighbourhood ministering angel.
Whether a chance meeting in the street
or following hot on the heels of a doctor's visit
she's onto anyone's infirmity with words of comfort.
'Don't despair yet. Some cases have recovered.'
'Luckily, not all those ugly scars will be permanent.'
'Really, the damage to your nose isn't too disfiguring.'
'If you are left with a limp after the bone heals,
I am sure you will cope with being disabled.'

A dose of flu has her in her element.
Invites herself in, 'to support you in your hour of need'
when left well provided and just wanting to sleep,
but whenever you drift off, her ear is on your chest
to be reassured that you are still breathing,
warning of pneumonia setting in with fatal results.
'When old Ted got it, his heart gave out
so you're lucky the hospital is just down the road,'
then she strengthens herself with your thermos tea
should emergency intervention be needed.

When her ministration runs its course,
she leaves with a sigh of benevolent satisfaction
so at last you can sink into the welcome arms of sleep,
and we are all aware of the danger of that!

Frustration

All I want is a stamp
and the post office queue slowly inches forward,
paying bills, buying cards and stencilled mugs,
sending parcels overseas, questioning the cost,
arranging for mail to be held over.
Ascertaining the relative merits of packaging,
discussing at length the meaning of fast delivery,
complaining about no delivery at all.
A passport photo is taken then eureka!
I step up to the counter and make my purchase.

It is now raining hard,
and with something more pressing on my mind
I am too hasty getting to the box outside
and fingers fumbling, the stamp flutters down,
retrieval thwarted by a fast flowing gutter
and damp to the core, I watch it flushed away.

So, what I need now is another stamp
and the post office queue slowly inches forward…

Contact

On my knees in the bedraggled front garden,
I am clearing away the mess after last night's storm
when there's a rustle
and I am eye to eye with a metre of lizard,
both of us suspended in the limbo of surprise.

I refocus, realise my endeavour is blocking the way
to its intended destination
so with fingers nervous of its beady-eyed scrutiny
and laser-flicking tongue, I relocate the obstruction.

Briefly, we resume our unexpected connection
then at warp speed
it skitters towards the escape hatch in the back fence
to the reptile nirvana of the bush,
the rest of its day much more promising than mine.

The Bond

After a phone call
with unhappy news
she suddenly appears
and jumps on my lap,
her body settling
against my chest,
deep vibrating purr
a comfort.
Gratefully I embrace
her familiar warmth
and she responds
with a whiskery caress.

But curled in sleep,
what had alerted her
to my distress?
Why did she decide
to offer support?
Which feline instinct
is sensing my frailty?

Emotions calmed,
I abandon speculation,
her motive clear,
and that old adage
Love isn't what you say
but what you do,
right on the money.

Tuning In

Eavesdropping can be an enthralling activity.
Even phone calls on the train that all can hear
whether we want to or not can be edifying
but confidences others aren't supposed to share
are definitely much more interesting,
more likely to make your day.
Like, 'Guess who I saw the boss with last night?'
'You really won't believe this but…'
and 'Don't tell anyone, but I've heard that…'

Actually, the covert eavesdrop is an art in itself.
Pretending to read in a waiting room,
examining the menu in a packed restaurant
or standing in a queue deep in thought
can be mastered with very little trouble
and you can learn stuff that 'nobody else knows',
who 'was seen cuddling in broad daylight'
or 'what Jackson was caught doing yesterday'.

So this is just between you and me when I divulge
the finer points of listening in, so make sure
that anyone nearby is really reading the paper,
concentrating on some digital device
or fussing around making afternoon tea
for we wouldn't want it to get out, would we?

A Very Satisfying Encounter

In the vast cavern of a pet and ponds store
a movement near my foot attracts my attention.
All eyes and legs, a small creature
is crawling towards sanctuary among the beds,
but perilously close to demise under my raised foot,
it halts its erratic progress
and rises up, full of aggression, eyes fixed on mine.

Catching my urgent waves, the owner arrives,
baffled by such an impatient summons
but when the nature of my distress is clear
she kneels down smiling broadly,
'So there you are,' she croons, scooping it up
and at breakneck speed, heads for the aquariums
on the far wall
with me, thrown into confusion, in their wake.

Gently eased into a tank it sinks to the bottom
and it seems that instead of delivering a lethal bite
I have frightened IT to death,
but pinhead bubbles begin spiralling
and I'm told with expressions of relief and delight
that it will survive its epic, overnight escape.
I had saved the life of a yabby
and not everyone can brag about that!

Wishful Thinking

Oh! to be in Iceland
now that summer's here,
living in an upmarket igloo,
the weather cold and clear.

Air-conditioned by nature,
no bills to struggle with,
bushfires cannot get me
and sunburn's just a myth.

I'd fish outside my door,
salmon steaks soon frying,
then, clad in furs I'd watch
the Northern Lights flying.

But our greenery I'd miss
and my daily sunshine fix,
while tennis in the snow
would clearly, never mix.

And those long dark hours
could be a problem when
after I've slept as usual,
how do I pass time then?

Perhaps if I stay at home
I can still end up a winner,
better off hot and sweaty
than a polar bear's dinner.

www.ingramcontent.com/pod-product-compliance
Lightning Source LLC
Chambersburg PA
CBHW062200100526
44589CB00014B/1885